AF448814

ODE TO THE
MOON

ABBY KAY

Ode to the

Moon

Abby Kay

Copyright © Kiona Assing 2023

This book may not be reproduced, transmitted, or stored by any means or in any form without the prior written consent of the publisher. This applies to all formats of this publication (electronic, mechanical, recording, or any other format).

All rights reserved. Published in the Republic of Trinidad and Tobago by Scarlet Ibis Publishing House Limited, Couva.

www.scarletibispublishing.com

ISBN 978-976-96581-3-4

Contents

2

Illuminating Night

Darkness reigns
Be afraid
Better yet pray to the Gods for
release from fear
When Ra sends protection
It doesn't calm the soul
It chills the core
As he uncovers all that lies before
Dread his power
Friend and foe
Under the cover of night
As he sneaks in
Speckles of light
Illuminating sin

Sneak Me the Sun

When the skies are dark, and the
Stars are too far
To give light
You sneak me the sun

Clouds try to hide you,
But you shine through
No matter where
In the dark I am
You sneak me some light

Neither of us have light of our own
But so I don't get lost in the dark
abyss
You sneak me some day

Salt Water

I sit on the shore
Contemplating how you
left me
Why did you go?
I can't survive this
Heart constricted
I have no more strength
The pressure builds up
Heaving my chest
Fighting for air
Salt Water, the only thing that
eases this pain
it flows
pulling the sorrow out of my soul
rolling down, unbidden
coming in waves
I wish it would wash me away
The agony of my grief mirrored in
the crashing of waves

Calmed only by the illumination of
the moon
Shining
Aglow with
The memory of
you
Sitting here
With me again
The waves still crashing
Salt water still flowing
But now a peace and stillness
My heart still beating

My Friend

The moon has become my
mentor,
My inspiration
My guide
She is there on the nights that I
look up in despair
Her presence calms me
It gives me peace
It gives me strength
Her standing there,
That ever-present beacon of light
Gives me freedom to shed my
previously concealed tears
All while building
Confidence in my ability
To overcome

The moon has become my saviour
She cradles my heart as I stare
into her light

I may never touch her surface
But she has touched my spirit

The moon has become my bed
mate
And I stare at her as I lay my head
to rest
As I play my soulful melody
And say my heartfelt prayer
I look at her
And think of us
What a pair we make
Sisters, or closer
Whatever you may call us
But I bless the day I could have
said
The moon became my friend

Dream Mother

Yemoja

Mother of the Seas

Help me

Heal me

Hear me

Please!

I know you speak

You deafen me in my dreams

Images flash and send my heart in torment

A warning

To guard

To protect

To defend

But please stay silent and listen to
me

    I hear you, child

Do you really?

Yemoja, mother, I meet you under
darkness's light

This is all that I want

    But you know it's not right

I know,

I know

I'm not sure I care

    *You will one day when you're
crying different tears*

*With your shroud coloured
lonely, I know it blinds you to see,
but I assuage your pain with this
promise from me*

*When your heart is heavy
again*

*Know that burden weighs
also on me*

Come to the darkness

And to the sea

Under the moonlight

Silence the cacophony

*Of discordance between your
wants and your needs*

*The truth will always be buried
in your dreams.*

Moon Moments

Forever told that the moon holds
magic

Full moon comes and

our spirits howl

My father gathered us, my sister
and I,

to hear the stories,

passed down from our ancestors,

modified specifically,

for our young ears

Stories of magic and wonder

and darkness and mystery.

I look to the moon and I'm
instantly transported,

back to the nights of my
memories

Back to climbing on

my father's back

as we look out the window and
pray to you.

O moon, O great Moon, O glorious
moon

I look to the moon and I hear

the stories of old replay in my
head

Stories of warning

to not run out in the dark,

stories of evil spirits

meant to lure away naughty
children, or

exact revenge on despicable men

Stories of bloodsuckers and
shapeshifters,

of the evil underbelly of human
nature

The stories play loudly in my mind
but

fear hesitates

to infiltrate my soul

for I am bathed in

protective light

O moon, O great moon, o glorious
moon

Gravity trips me and I fall to the
earth,

I know what has called me

to remember my prayers

I know, that which guides me in
the dark

Can cause a stumble in the light

Lesson learnt

Humility restored

I know what force keeps us all
grounded on this hospitable
planet,

what keeps us from being ripped
away

and disintegrated

returned to mere dust

floating in space

I know the power,

And I know what wields it

and I pay homage right there on
the floor

Then I garner the strength to

get up once more

O moon, O great moon, O glorious
moon

Goddess of creativity,

of writers, of poetry

Goddess of emotions, creating
havoc in

a chaotic mind

...

LUNA

...

Call me

LUNAtic

As I revel and rejoice in

LUNAcy

See me push and pull

My heart

Like waves

Disturb the peace,

Till the soil

In the newness of

The first quarter, plant

The seeds

O moon, O great moon, O glorious
moon

Sweet symbol of Fertility

Spawn me new inspiration

Fertile mind, fertile

womb, fertile

ground, fertile

heart

When you are full, I fill

up to the brim until,

At last

To fruition

O moon, O great moon, O glorious
moon

I take this moon moment to show
gratitude to you.

A Mother's Love

I give the moon my sadness
I share with it my fears
Under the cloak of darkness
It sheds light on all my tears

When my heart is heavy
Gravity pulls at my pain
Selene's price it shall levy
Yet it eases most of my strain

I cry under the moonlight
It sends magic to my dreams
I know in those moments that
I too am a daughter of Selene

The Moon, the Yoni,
and Water

Light in the darkness

Bringing gravity and tide

Infusing this body of water

With waves of pleasure,

Rippling through

This blood

This bone

This sinew

Sustainer of life

Thirst quenching solvent

Under the night's spotlight

Refresh this earthly being

Wash this body clean

Boil with this desire

Cool with this release

Gateway of life

Symbol of fertility

Awash with the light of Selene

Waves of desire boiling up to a
peak

Gushing forth and shaking this
body in release

Birthing a wish

Into reality

The moon's pull

Infused into water,

Birthed through the yoni

Wields incredible power

Birth now this wish

Bring forth this request

Release from this centre

My coveted desire

I call on the power

The Moon, The Yoni, and Water

Bless the womb

Barren woman cries

Each time she

Copulates

Please, she begs

Let this bear fruit

All she wants is

A love that can't be

Stripped away

To prove her womanhood and

Someone to reign

Her love upon, and

Almost certainly

Love her back

In the darkness, save for your light

Barren woman cries

Mother of mine

Please let me be

A mother to my own

One,

Two

Or three

Bless this womb

Laying bare inside me

Ode to the Moon

o moon, o great moon
o merciful and powerful moon
shining in your brilliance
you broker no defiance

you alone command my soul
your wonders I will forever extol
leave me awash with your
blessings forever
and I shall reside in darkness never

o moon o glorious moon
shining light into the darkness
lure with your light

*make the waves crash upon the
earth and help the tide find its way
home*

calm the spirits

excite the soul

fill my life

lead me home

home to where

my heart belongs.

to what excites and fuels my soul

release from within me

the spirit of all that I

innately should be

release my power

from these earthly confines

be with me in the darkness

light my way home

o beautiful moon

I spread my arms wide

spinning wildly in your glow

merciful moon

the sun shines on you

you shine on me

reflect the brilliance of my soul

remind me that light is

from the sun, the stars

and also my heart

o moon o glorious moon

o precious and irreplaceable moon

*thank you for being the light in my
darkest days*

thank you for guiding

in dreams and vibrations

*thank you for fertilizing the
passions of my mind*

o moon o glorious moon

o merciful moon

*I've gained perspective through
you*

my emotions,

tumultuous at first

war against their selfish wants

in defense of my undesirable
needs

now need wins

o moon o glorious moon

o precious and irreplaceable moon

clouds pass to obscure your
brilliance, but

it only reveals a ringed rainbow

as your light refracts and I cannot
help but see

that so is it with me

when obstacles come that dim my
light and hide my wonder

it merely reveals

a beauty that forms

a protective ring of

my inner light

*revealing the blessings and
protection around me*

o moon, o great moon

individual of light

bothered and bent

seen through obscurity,

I stand for beauty

I see the light

I shine light

my beauty will never be hidden,

only magnified

only shown in a different sphere

in different colours

but still mine

it still shines through

I learnt that from you

o moon

o merciful moon

o glorious moon

I see on your surface

many forms and figures

and they change like my soul changes

adaptable

sometimes your face reflects imperfections or turmoil

hidden within

but it never loses its brilliance

for even in flaws I see...

beauty

and when the clouds thicken

determined to

obscure my view

the light may be dimmed and
struggle to find its way through

but

it finds its way through

as difficult as it may be

it finds its way through

o moon, o glorious moon

o merciful moon

not just my brilliance I see in you

I see the light shining from those I
love

living their lives,

unapologetically

their light shines my way home

under your glow

I reflect on these wonders

flooded with your light

my mind finds peace

o moon

o glorious moon

o merciful moon

I send these words to you

out of more than just gratitude

out of love

and of faithfulness

may this be a promise

to myself

that I will never lose sight of the brilliance

that is you,

that is me

may I never lose sight that

my light

can be reflected and

it can make waves and

it can guide the way

o moon, o glorious moon

o merciful moon

thank you

Full Moon Magic

I know it scares you when the
crazies come out

Howling and praying and dancing
in the silence

For 3 days its magic will reign

Full moon

Full throttle

Full of happiness and pain

It spells success for those who
dare

To call on its power

Full moon magic is here

Crescent moon

Crescent moon keeping

Peaceful watch

As we reap the harvest and

Fertilize new crop

Crescent moon on a

starry night

marks the time when

we transplant from

a field of fear

to one of love

Born under the waning crescent

Foreday morning

Crisp cool air

Damsel in distress

Waddles down the hill in search

Of a hero

To take her to the house

Where the healers reside

To deliver her little miracle

Who will soon suck at her breast

As she was driven

Light, not yet on the horizon

Breathing through the pain

The waning crescent energy

Helped her sustain

A rising pain

The rising sun

Breathe

Breathe

Breathe

Now push!

Come on mommy

Push again

Definitely not easy

But not crippling pain

She birthed a beauty

But was so dismayed

The nurse said she was healthy

Mommy cried and looked away

I'm glad she's healthy but

I wanted a boy

She didn't yet realise

She had birthed joy

Born into honour

Born into wealth

Under the waning crescent

Brown Hills

Reborn again.

About the Author

Abby Kay is the nom de plume of Ms. Kiona Assing. Kiona is a certified project manager with a background in civil engineering. She is a business owner, tutor, and coach; however, she has always harboured a love for writing and the arts.

Her natural inner joy is always multiplied when mixed with good food, great music, dance, and loving friends and family.

Follow her on social media for the latest updates and news on upcoming releases at:

Facebook Page: Kiona Assing – Abby Kay

Instagram: @msabbykay

Website: msabbykay.com

www.ingramcontent.com/pod-product-compliance
Lightning Source LLC
Chambersburg PA
CBHW051504140726
47987CB00006B/2872